Lexile: _____480 L_____

AR/BL: _____2.7_____

AR Points: _____0.5_____

Diggin' Dirt

Science Adventures with Kitanai the Origami Dog

by Thomas Kingsley Troupe

illustrated by Jamey Christoph

PICTURE WINDOW BOOKS
a capstone imprint

Mikio was taking a break from his gardening.
To relax, he folded an origami dog.

"You are almost done, my friend. You're a fine hound, worthy to explore my garden. I shall call you Kitanai."

Kitanai jumped down into the garden.
His nose perked up.

"what IS that incredible smell? I have to find it!"

Kitanai took a step,
then he stopped.

"oh, great! LOOK at my poor paws!
what IS this stuff?"

"That, my friend, is Earth's most precious resource," a nearby voice said. "That's dirt!"

"Who's there?" Kitanai growled. He turned and found an earthworm curled on the ground.

"Welcome to the garden. I'm Roger."

Kitanai looked around. Dirt was everywhere!
He tried to wipe off his paws in the dirt, but he
only made them dirtier.

"HOW can this dirt stuff
be so precious? It just
seems SO ... filthy!"

"Gardeners and farmers usually call dirt by a different name—SOIL. Life on Earth depends on healthy soil."

"The top layer of dirt you're walking on is called topsoil. It contains many of the nutrients and water that plants need to grow. Plants create food for humans and animals to eat. So soil is the reason people and animals have food."

"No food, no life. I get it!"

"So **where** do the nutrients in soil come from?" asked Kitanai.

"Do you see all the rotting plant and animal matter in the topsoil? That's called **humus**. Humus, along with other things such as water, air, minerals, and bug droppings, helps plants grow."

"I'm stepping on **dead critters** and **bug poop? GROSS!**"

"**Not gross at all.**" Roger said. "All that material breaks down to create **new dirt.**"

Kitanai could smell the strange scent again. "**I must find what's buried out here!**" Kitanai howled.

"**See you later, Roger!**"

The sky grew dark, and rain began to fall. Kitanai took shelter beneath a plant. He found Roger nearby, snacking on a fallen leaf.

"How'd you get here so fast?"

"simple," said Roger. "I make awesome tunnels, Kitanai. The tunnels help me get around, but they help the soil too."

"Help the soil? But aren't you destroying it?" Kitanai asked.

"No. As I tunnel, I poop. My waste is eaten by fungi and bacteria. They're called decomposers. Decomposers help break down materials to make soil healthy."

"WOW," Kitanai said. "ICK!"

Roger slipped down into his tunnel. Kitanai peered into it.

"Our tunnels also let **rainwater** and **air** go deeper into the soil. This helps all the fungi and bacteria that live in the soil survive."

"I don't see any **fungi** or **bacteria**," said Kitanai.

"They're too small to see with just your eyes," Roger said. "You'd need a **really** powerful microscope to see them."

Kitanai caught another whiff of that scent. The scent was close by! He walked in a circle through the mud, stopped, and started to dig.

"Hey, that's good! Digging in the dirt is great for the soil. It helps mix the topsoil with the next layer of dirt. Moles, prairie dogs, and other animals that live underground do most of the digging."

"Oh, really? I just want to find whatever is buried out here!"

"The dirt down here is **different**," Kitanai said. "It's not as **dark** and **fluffy** as the topsoil."

"You've dug down to the **subsoil layer**. There's less humus and more rock than in the topsoil. In a few thousand years, the rocks will break down and become part of the topsoil."

"You mean Earth is making **new dirt?**"

"You got it. It just keeps **recycling** itself. Dirt has been Earth's skin for **hundreds of millions of years.**"

Kitanai kept digging. Soon he wagged his tail happily and hopped out of the pit.

"It was a bone! It was down there pretty deep, on top of a big layer of rock!"

"Bedrock. That layer is solid rock. No one gets past that. Not without a **big machine**."

"you sure know a lot about dirt, Roger," Kitanai said.

"Dirt is my home. I love it," said Roger. "And you should too. You've really lived up to your name today."

"what do you mean?" Kitanai asked.

"Don't you know what Kitanai means in Japanese?" asked Roger. Kitanai shook his head.

Roger smiled like only an earthworm could. "It means 'dirty'!"

GLOSSARY

bacteria—very small living things that are found in soil; bacteria are decomposers

decomposer—a living thing, such as bacteria and fungi, that feeds on dead plants and animals and turns them into soil

fungus—a living thing similar to a plant, but without flowers or leaves

humus—the wet, dark part of soil that is made of rotting plants and animals; humus has nutrients that plants need

mineral—a material found in nature that is not an animal or a plant

nutrient—a part of food, like a vitamin, that is used for growth

origami—the Japanese art of paper folding

subsoil—a layer of rock or soil beneath the surface of the ground

topsoil—the dark surface layer of soil in which plants grow

READ MORE

Aloian, Molly. *Different Kinds of Soil.* Everybody Digs Soil. New York: Crabtree Pub. Co., 2009.

Lindbo, David, et. al. and Judy Mannes. *Soil!: Get the Inside Scoop.* Madison, Wisc.: Soil Science Society of America, 2008.

Schuh, Mari. *Soil Basics.* Science Builders. Mankato, Minn.: Capstone Press, 2012.

MAKE AN ORIGAMI DOG

Kitanai is one dirty pup! Want to make your own paper pooch? Check out these instructions to make an origami dog.

what you need

origami paper
markers

WHAT YOU DO

Folds

valley folds are shown with a dashed line. One side of the paper is folded against the other like a book. A sharp fold is made by running your finger along the fold line.

mountain folds are shown with a white dashed and dotted line. The paper should be folded sharply behind the model.

Arrows

single-pointed arrow:
Fold the paper in the direction of the arrow.

double-pointed arrow:
Fold the paper and then unfold it.

half-pointed arrow:
Fold the paper behind.

1. Start with the colored side of the paper face down. Valley fold the top point to the bottom point.

2. Valley fold the left point to the right point and unfold.

3. Valley fold the left and right points down. Allow the points to rest to the left and right of the center fold.

4. Mountain fold the top and bottom points behind the model.

5. Turn the model over. Now give your pup a friendly face!

INDEX

Read all the books in the series:

Diggin' Dirt: Science Adventures with Kitanai the Origami Dog

Let's Rock!: Science Adventures with Rudie the Origami Dinosaur

Magnet Power!: Science Adventures with MAG-3000 the Origami Robot

Plant Parts Smarts: Science Adventures with Charlie the Origami Bee

Thanks to our advisers for their expertise, research, and advice:
Paul McDaniel, Professor of Soil Science
Soil & Land Resources Division
University of Idaho

Terry Flaherty, PhD, Professor of English
Minnesota State University, Mankato

Editor: Shelly Lyons
Designer: Ashlee Suker
Art Director: Nathan Gassman
Production Specialist: Eric Manske
The illustrations in this book were created digitally.

Picture Window Books are published by Capstone,
1710 Roe Crest Drive, North Mankato, Minnesota 56003
www.capstonepub.com

Library of Congress Cataloging-in-Publication Data
Troupe, Thomas Kingsley.
Diggin' dirt : science adventures with Kitanai the origami dog /
by Thomas Kingsley Troupe ; illustrated by Jamey Christoph.
pages cm. — (Origami science adventures)
Audience: K to grade 3
ISBN 978-1-4048-7969-0 (library binding)
ISBN 978-1-4048-8066-5 (paperback)
ISBN 978-1-4795-0000-0 (eBook PDF)
1. Natural history—Juvenile literature. 2. Origami—Juvenile literature. I. Christoph, James, illustrator. II. Title.
QH48.T85 2013
508—dc23   2012029511

Photo credits:
Digital illustrations include royalty-free images from iStock and Shutterstock.
Capstone Studio/Karon Dubke, 22–23

INTERNET SITES

FactHound offers a safe, fun way to find Internet sites related to this book. All of the sites on FactHound have been researched by our staff.

Here's all you do:

Visit www.facthound.com

Type in this code: 9781404879690

Super-cool stuff!
Check out projects, games and lots more at
www.capstonekids.com

Printed in the United States of America in Brainerd, Minnesota.
092012   006938BANGS13